The Hound of the Baskervilles

written by Sir Arthur Conan Doyle
adapted by Ruth Dowley

illustrated by Victor Tavares

3

Incredible Adventures

Contents

Rigby is an imprint of Pearson Education Limited, a company incorporated in England and Wales, having its registered office at Edinburgh Gate, Harlow, Essex, CM20 2JE. Registered company number: 872828

www.rigbyed.co.uk

Help and support for teachers, plus the widest range of education solutions

Rigby is a registered trademark of Reed Elsevier Inc, Licensed to Pearson Education Limited

Incredible Adventures first published 2004

'The Hound of the Baskervilles' © Ruth Dowley 2004
'The Stowaways' © Roger McGough. Reprinted by permission of The Peters Fraser and Dunlop Group Limited on behalf of: Roger McGough
'Gulliver's Travels' © Steve Barlow and Steve Skidmore 2004

Series editor: Shirley Bickler

11

10

Incredible Adventures
ISBN 9780433035398

Group reading pack with teaching notes
ISBN 9780433035701

Illustrated by Victor Tavares, Leanne Jackson and Alan Down

Cover illustration © Peter Greenwood

Designed by StoreyBooks

Repro by Digital Imaging, Glasgow

Printed and bound in China(CTPS/10)

This is a story about the famous Victorian detective, Sherlock Holmes. It is told by his friend, Dr Watson.

Sir Charles Baskerville was found dead on the edge of Dartmoor. The official report said that he had died of a weak heart. But his heir, Henry Baskerville, was not so sure. The footprints of a giant hound were found near Sir Charles' body. His face was twisted with fear.

Sir Henry asked Sherlock Holmes to investigate the case.

***

"My Uncle Charles believed a curse hangs over the Baskerville family," said Sir Henry. "Long ago, another member of our family was found dead on the moor. A huge black hound was tearing at his throat. Its eyes blazed and its jaws dripped fire.

Uncle Charles saw the same dreadful hound on the moor several times before he died," he went on. "So did other people. It glowed like a fiend from hell."

"Do you believe this hound to be supernatural?" asked Holmes.

"I do not know, but nothing is going to stop me going to my family home!" Sir

Henry replied stoutly. "Look, I have been sent this letter."

Words had been cut out and glued onto plain paper. "Keep away from the moor," they warned.

Holmes examined the print. "This is cut from *The Times*. I suspect it comes from an educated person. Tell me, who would inherit the Baskerville fortune if something happened to you?"

"As far as I know, I am the last Baskerville," said Sir Henry. "I had a younger uncle, but he died of yellow fever in Central America."

"Has anything else strange occurred since you arrived in London?" asked Holmes.

"I bought some new boots. Before I wore them, one was stolen. Then it was found. Now one of my old shoes is missing!"

Holmes leaned forward. "Most interesting." He turned to me. "Watson, I would like you to go with Sir Henry to Baskerville Hall and stay close to him whenever he goes out."

"I will, with pleasure," I said. I love an adventure.

From the station, a wagon carried us across the bleak moor to Baskerville Hall. It was a gloomy place covered in ivy. Inside, dark shadows filled the corners of oak-panelled rooms.

Next morning, Sir Henry busied himself with papers. I walked along the edge of the moor to the post office to send my first report to Holmes. On the way, I met a gentleman with a butterfly net. It was Mr Stapleton who lived with his sister two miles from Baskerville Hall.

He warned me about the dangerous mire in the middle of the moor. "Many animals get sucked down to their deaths there," he said.

As we spoke, a long, moaning howl swept over the moor. It swelled to a roar before sinking away. A chill of fear seized my heart.

"What is that?" I cried.

"The locals say it is the Hound of the Baskervilles calling for its prey," said Stapleton.

A rare butterfly flew past us. Stapleton excused himself to chase after it.

8

While I waited, a beautiful dark-haired woman came from the direction of his house. I guessed it was his sister and raised my hat.

"Go back!" she said in a low voice. "Go straight back to London!"

I stared at her. "Why should I?"

"Believe me, Sir Henry! The moor is not safe for you!"

"You mistake me. I am not Sir Henry. I am only his humble friend, Dr Watson."

She looked vexed. "I am so sorry. Please forget what I have said."

"Is it the curse that makes you fearful for Sir Henry?" I pressed.

"It is only that I was shocked by Sir Charles' death and felt the new heir should be warned. I beg you not to tell my brother of my foolishness."

Stapleton returned from chasing the butterfly. His eyes darted from his sister to me, but he chatted lightly of a school he had run in the north.

Over the next week, Sir Henry made friends with Mr Stapleton. He was soon in love with Stapleton's beautiful sister.

Then Holmes arrived at the Hall and told Sir Henry, "I must take Watson back to London for a few days."

Sir Henry's face grew long. "This will be a lonely place on my own. I have heard strange howling on the moor. Besides, Dr Watson and I are to dine with the Stapletons this evening."

"You must go without him, Sir Henry," said Holmes. I was greatly surprised when he added, "and I would like you to walk back across the moor alone."

"But that is the very thing you have told me not to do!" cried Sir Henry.

"My dear fellow, trust me," said Holmes.

Looking anxious, Sir Henry agreed.

"Make sure that you walk along the track that leads from the Stapleton's house," Holmes told him.

Holmes and I left. However, instead of going to London, we waited till nightfall and secretly returned to the moor. A dense white fog hung over the great mire in its centre.

We crept up the track and hid behind rocks near Stapleton's house. I pointed out the bright lights of the dining room.

"That is where Sir Henry will be with Stapleton and his sister."

"She is not his sister," revealed Holmes. "I made enquiries in the north where he had his school. The lady is his wife."

"What! Why the pretence?"

"He wanted Sir Henry to fall in love with her in order to lure him into visits such as this."

The fog drifted towards the house. Holmes grew agitated. "If Sir Henry doesn't come soon, we will lose sight of the path."

13

But the fog crept around the house and on towards us. To keep our view of the path, we were forced to hide further back. We waited anxiously.

At last we heard Sir Henry. He stepped clear of the thick bank of fog and hurried past. We went on glaring into the cloud.

Holmes cocked his pistol. "Look out! It's coming!"

14

We gasped. Out of the fog sprung a terrifying creature. A hound it was, black and huge, but not one mortal eyes should ever see. Fire burst from its mouth. Its eyes glowed. It was outlined in flickering flames.

With savage bounds, the fiend leapt after Sir Henry. Holmes and I fired together. It howled, but tore on.

As we raced up the track, Sir Henry screamed. We saw that the hound had him down!

Instantly, Holmes fired again. With a hideous roar, the dreadful beast fell dead upon its side.

We helped Sir Henry to a rock. Thank God, he was not hurt, though quaking with fright. Even now, the jaws of the hound seemed to drip fire.

I touched them. My fingers gleamed in the darkness. "Phosphorus!"

"A cunning preparation of phosphorus," agreed Holmes. "It has no smell to interfere with the scent of the prey. You see, that is why Stapleton needed to steal a boot Sir Henry had *worn*. It gave the hound his scent. But come! We must be after the villain!"

Holmes and I rushed back down the track to the house. There was no sign of Stapleton, but upstairs we found a locked room. Holmes kicked in the lock, and the door flew open.

Gagged and tied to a post was Mrs Stapleton. When we undid her, we saw that she had been beaten.

"The brute!" cried Holmes.

She wept. "It was for the inheritance. My husband is Sir Henry's heir. He is the son of Sir Henry's younger uncle who died in Central America. He set the hound after Sir Charles to kill him, but poor Sir Charles died of heart failure before he was attacked. Then only Sir Henry stood in the way."

"So you sent the letter to Sir Henry to warn him."

"Yes. And when my husband saw I would not go along with his plans this evening, he tied me here."

"Tell us where he is hiding," pressed Holmes.

"He will have gone to the old mine in the mire where he kept the hound."

"He will be sucked down to his death!" I said. "No one could find a safe path through the mire in this fog!"

And so it proved. Stapleton was never seen again. When we searched in the morning, all we found was Sir Henry's old boot, thrown away as Stapleton fled.

Stapleton and the curse of the Baskervilles were both at an end.

The Stowaways

written by Roger McGough

illustrated by Leanne Jackson

When I lived in Liverpool, my best friend was a boy called Midge. Kevin Midgeley was his real name, but we called him Midge for short. And he was short, only about three cornflake boxes high (empty ones at that). No three ways about it. Midge was my best friend and we had lots of things in common. Things we enjoyed doing like … climbing trees, playing footy, going to the movies, hitting each other really hard. And there were things we didn't enjoy doing like … sums, washing behind our ears, eating cabbage.

But there was one thing that really bound us together, one thing we had in common – a love of the sea.

In the old days (but not so long ago), the river Mersey was far busier than it is today. Those were the days of the great passenger liners and cargo boats. Large ships sailed out of Liverpool for Canada, the United States, South Africa, the West Indies, all over the world. My father had been to sea and so had all my uncles, and my grandfather. Six foot six. Muscles rippling in the wind, huge hands grappling with the helm, rum-soaked and fierce as a wounded shark (and that was only my grandmother!) By the time they were twenty, most young men in this city had visited parts of the globe I can't even spell.

In my bedroom each night, I used to lie in bed (best place to lie really), I used to lie there, especially in winter, and listen to the foghorns being sounded all down the river. I could picture the ship nosing its way out of the docks into the channel and out into the Irish Sea. It was exciting. All those exotic places. All those exciting adventures.

Midge and I knew what we wanted to do when we left school…become sailors. A captain, an admiral, perhaps one day even a steward. Of course we were only about seven or eight at the time so we thought we'd have a long time to wait. But oddly enough, the call of the sea came sooner than we'd expected.

It was a Wednesday night if I remember rightly. I never liked Wednesdays for some reason. I could never spell it for a start and it always seemed to be raining, and there were still two days to go before the weekend. Anyway, Midge and I got into trouble at school. I don't remember what for (something trivial I suppose like chewing gum in class, forgetting how to read, setting fire to the music teacher), I forget now. But we were picked on, nagged, told off and all those boring things that grown-ups get up to sometimes.

26

And, of course, to make matters worse, my mum and dad were in a right mood when I got home. Nothing to do with me, of course, because as you have no doubt gathered by now, I was the perfect child: clean, well-mannered, obedient… soft in the head. But for some reason I was clipped round the ear and sent to bed early for being childish. Childish! I ask you. I *was* a child. A child acts his age, what does he get? Wallop!

So that night in bed, I decided… Yes, you've guessed it. I could hear the big ships calling out to each other as they sidled out of the Mersey into the oceans beyond. The tugs leading the way like proud little guide dogs. That's it. We'd run away to sea, Midge and I. I'd tell him the good news in the morning.

27

The next two days just couldn't pass quickly enough for us. We had decided to begin our amazing around-the-world voyage on Saturday morning so that in case we didn't like it we would be back in time for school on Monday. As you can imagine there was a lot to think about – what clothes to take, how much food and drink. We decided on two sweaters each and wellies in case we ran into storms around Cape Horn. I read somewhere that sailors lived off rum and dry biscuits, so I poured some of my dad's into an empty pop bottle, and borrowed a handful of half-coated chocolate digestives.

I also packed my lonestar cap gun and Midge settled on a magnifying glass.

On Friday night we met round at his house to make the final plans. He lived with his granny and his sister, so there were no nosy parents to discover what we were up to. We hid all the stuff in the shed in the yard and arranged to meet outside his back door next morning at the crack of dawn, or sunrise – whichever came first.

Sure enough, Saturday morning, when the big finger was on twelve and the little one was on six, Midge and I met with our little bundles under our arms and ran up the street as fast as our tiptoes could carry us.

Hardly anyone was about, and the streets were so quiet and deserted except for a few pigeons straddling home after all-night parties. It was a very strange feeling, as if we were the only people alive and the city belonged entirely to us. And soon the world would be ours as well – once we'd stowed away on a ship bound for somewhere far off and exciting.

By the time we'd got down to the Pier Head, though, a lot more people were up and about, including a policeman who eyed us suspiciously. "Ello, Ello, Ello," he said, "and where are you two going so early in the morning?"

"Fishing," I said.

"Train spotting," said Midge, and we looked at each other.

"Just so long as you're not running away to sea."

"Oh no," we chorused. "Just as if."

He winked at us. "Off you go then, and remember to look both ways before crossing your eyes."

31

We ran off and straight down on to the landing stage where a lot of ships were tied up. There was no time to lose because already quite a few were putting out to sea, their sirens blowing, the hundreds of seagulls squeaking excitedly, all tossed into the air like giant handfuls of confetti.

Then I noticed a small ship just to the left where the crew were getting ready to cast off. They were so busy doing their work that it was easy for Midge and me to slip on board unnoticed. Up the gang-plank we went and straight up on to the top deck where there was nobody around. The sailors were all busy down below, hauling in the heavy ropes and revving up the engine that turned the great propellers.

We looked around for somewhere to hide. "I know, let's climb down the funnel," said Midge.

"Great idea," I said, taking the mickey. "Or, better still, let's disguise ourselves as a pair of seagulls and perch up there on the mast."

32

Then I spotted them. The lifeboats. "Quick, let's climb into one of those, they'll never look in there — not unless we run into icebergs anyway." So in we climbed, and no sooner had we covered ourselves with the tarpaulin than there was a great shuddering and the whole ship seemed to turn round on itself. We were off! Soon we'd be digging for diamonds in the Brazilian jungle or building sandcastles on a tropical island. But we had to be patient, we knew that. Those places are a long way away, it could take days, even months.

So we were patient. Very patient. Until after
what seemed like hours and hours we decided to
eat our rations, which I divided up equally. I gave
Midge all the rum and I had all the biscuits. Looking
back on it now, that probably wasn't a good idea,
especially for Midge.

What with the rolling of the ship and not
having had any breakfast, and the excitement, and a
couple of swigs of rum – well you can guess what
happened – woooorrppp! All
over the place. We pulled
back the sheet and
decided to give
ourselves up. We were
too far away at sea
now for the captain to
turn back. The worst he
could do was to clap us
in iron or shiver our
timbers.

We climbed down on to the deck and as Midge staggered to the nearest rail to feed the fishes, I looked out to sea hoping to catch sight of a whale, a shoal of dolphins, perhaps see the coast of America coming in to view. And what did I see? The Liver Buildings.

Anyone can make a mistake can't they? I mean, we weren't to know we'd stowed away on a ferryboat.

One that goes from Liverpool to Birkenhead and back again, toing and froing across the Mersey. We'd done four trips hidden in the lifeboat and ended up back in Liverpool. And we'd only been away about an hour and a half. "Ah well, so much for running away to sea," we thought as we disembarked (although disembowelled might be a better word as far as Midge was concerned). Rum? Yuck.

37

We got the bus home. My mum and dad were having their breakfast. "Aye, aye," said my dad, "here comes the early bird. And what have you been up to then?"

"I ran away to sea," I said.

"Mm, that's nice," said my mum, shaking out the cornflakes. "That's nice."

38

Gulliver's Travels

The First Part: A Voyage to Lilliput

By Jonathan Swift
retold by Steve Barlow
and Steve Skidmore
illustrated by Alan Down

In this year of Our Lord 1699, I became ship's doctor on board the *Antelope*. On May 4th, we set sail from Bristol bound for the East Indies.

Goodbye, children. Take care of your mother.

At first, our voyage went well...

...but, after six months at sea, we were caught in a violent storm. The seamen spied a rock. They shouted a warning. But the wind was so strong that we were driven upon it.

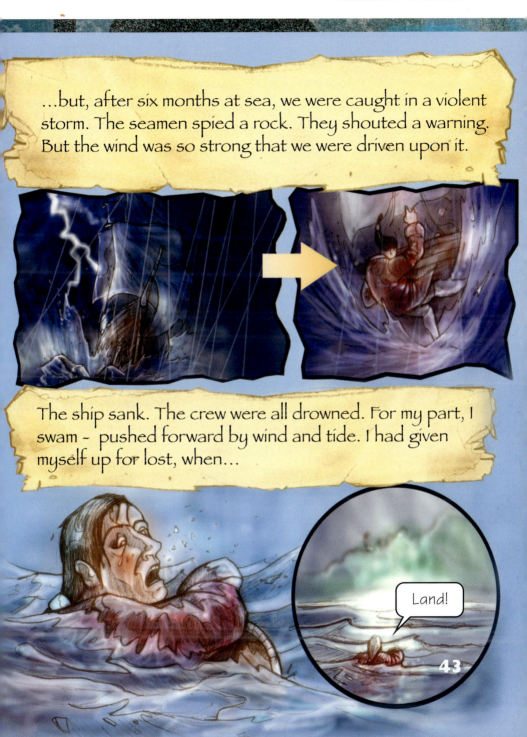

The ship sank. The crew were all drowned. For my part, I swam - pushed forward by wind and tide. I had given myself up for lost, when...

Land!

I was washed up on a beach, from where I crawled to safety. I lay down and slept more soundly than ever I had done in my life.

When I awoke I found I could not move. I could see only the sky. In a little time, I felt something alive moving on my left leg. The thing crept up my chest…

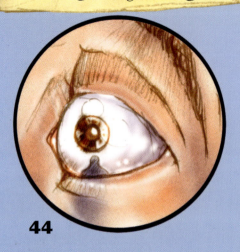

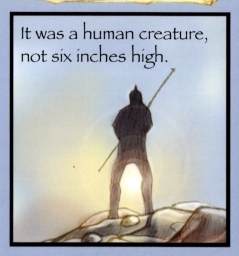

It was a human creature, not six inches high.

44

I felt above a hundred arrows strike my left hand – which pricked me like so many needles.

After this, I thought it wise to lie still. As I lay groaning with grief and pain, one of the little people began to speak. I could not understand what he said, but I afterwards learnt that his name was Secretary Reldresal, and that he spoke for his master, the Emperor of Lilliput.

47

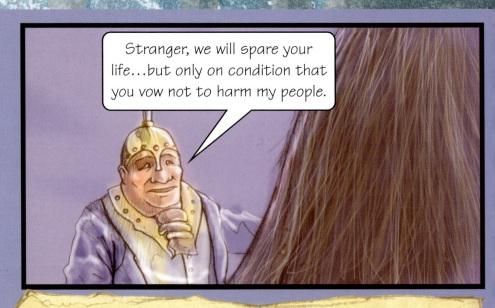

As soon as the Emperor had spoken, a furious argument broke out. Secretary Reldresal later explained to me that the Prime Minister, Flimnap, and the High Admiral wanted to get rid of me.

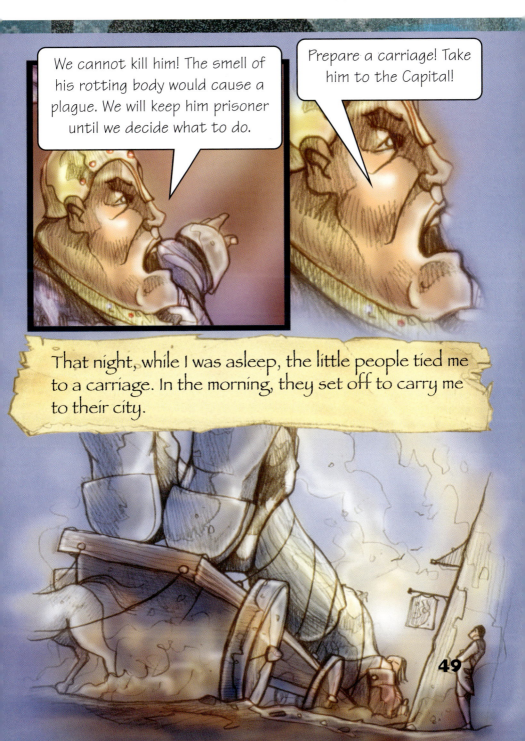

We cannot kill him! The smell of his rotting body would cause a plague. We will keep him prisoner until we decide what to do.

Prepare a carriage! Take him to the Capital!

That night, while I was asleep, the little people tied me to a carriage. In the morning, they set off to carry me to their city.

49

After several hours of travelling, my captors brought me to an ancient temple outside the city walls. The little people halted there. They untied me from the carriage and brought me victuals and drink.

The Man-Mountain will eat us out of house and home!

I ate legs and shoulders of lamb - two or three at a mouthful. The people were full of wonder and astonishment at my bulk and appetite!

After I had eaten, the soldiers made me understand that I was to crawl inside the temple. I could scarcely do more than lie down inside it.

Over the days that followed, the temple became my home. Still the little people were wary of me. They kept me in chains and I was very lonely and unhappy. Only Secretary Reldresal came often to visit me. He became my only friend in Lilliput.

Man-Mountain, if you are to live among us, you must learn our language.
The name of our land is Lilliput.

Lil - li - put...

As time passed, and I learned to speak their language, the people of Lilliput grew less afraid of me.

51

One day, while the Emperor's soldiers were examining the contents of my pockets, Reldresal arrived looking very upset.

Friend, why do you look so sad?

Terrible news, Man-Mountain. We are at war with the Empire c Blefuscu!

But why are the people of Blefuscu your enemies?

They insist that we must open our eggs at the big end.

It is terrible to think of such a thing. All the world knows that eggs should be opened at the small end!

What?

52

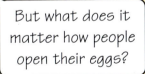

But what does it matter how people open their eggs?

What does it matter? Are you mad? I'm not standing around to listen to this. The people of Lilliput would rather die than open their eggs at the wrong end!

Friend Reldresal! Wait!

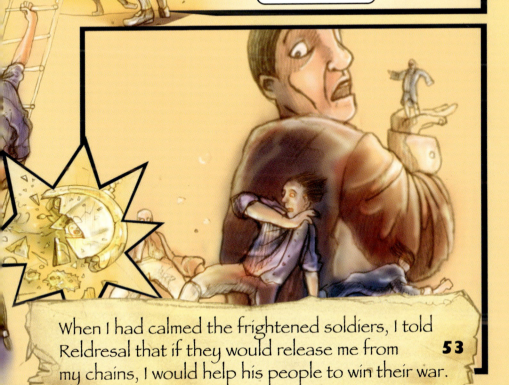

When I had calmed the frightened soldiers, I told Reldresal that if they would release me from my chains, I would help his people to win their war.

53

The Empire of Blefuscu was an island situated to the north-north-east side of Lilliput. The rival Empires were parted only by a channel of eight hundred yards wide. I learnt from the sailors that the water between Lilliput and Blefuscu was only seventy *glumgluffs* deep – shallow enough for me to wade across.

Their fleet is nearly ready to sail.

Don't worry. I have a plan.

I stepped into the water and waded across the strait between the islands. The water came only to my waist. The people of Lilliput lined the shore, their eyes followed my every move.

The Blefuscan sailors were speechless with astonishment and terror. As I approached their harbour, they ran for their lives.

55

56

When I towed the greatest ships of the Blefuscan fleet back to Lilliput, I was greeted with joy. As a reward for my services, the Emperor himself made me a Nardac – a Great Lord of Lilliput.

Unfortunately, not everyone was happy at my success...

57

One night, about two months later, I had another opportunity to do His Majesty a signal service. I was alarmed at midnight with the cries of many hundred people at my door. Something terrible had happened – the Emperor's palace was on fire! I got up in an instant, and hurried to the palace to see what I could do.

This is no good – these buckets don't hold enough water to put out the fire.

It seemed that this magnificent palace would be burnt down to the ground.

But at that moment, I had a brilliant idea.

Stand back!

I've never seen anyone put out a fire that way before!

Oh, no! What is he doing?

The flames died down in an instant, and the palace was saved! I thought the Emperor would be grateful for what I had done. Instead, he was angry. The Empress said she could never live in the palace again. I soon realized that they would never forgive me.

59

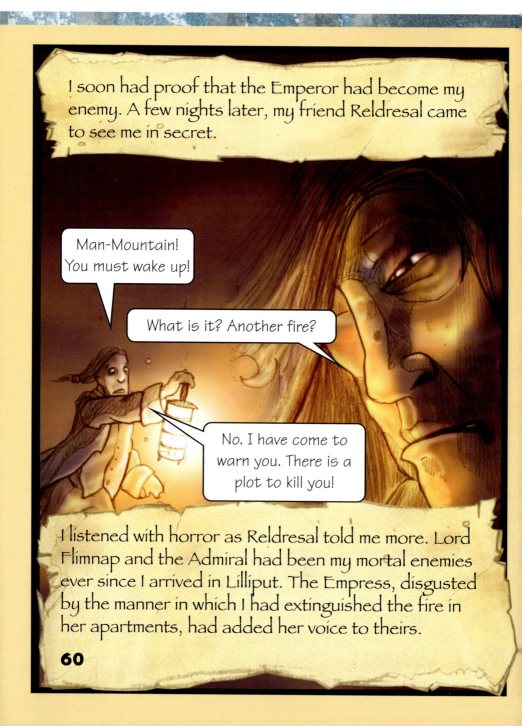

I soon had proof that the Emperor had become my enemy. A few nights later, my friend Reldresal came to see me in secret.

Man-Mountain! You must wake up!

What is it? Another fire?

No. I have come to warn you. There is a plot to kill you!

I listened with horror as Reldresal told me more. Lord Flimnap and the Admiral had been my mortal enemies ever since I arrived in Lilliput. The Empress, disgusted by the manner in which I had extinguished the fire in her apartments, had added her voice to theirs.

60

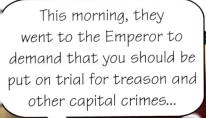

This morning, they went to the Emperor to demand that you should be put on trial for treason and other capital crimes...

Set fire to his temple! Burn him alive!

Shoot him with poisoned arrows!

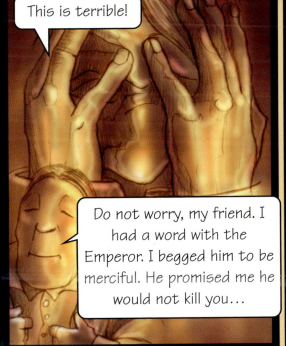

This is terrible!

Do not worry, my friend. I had a word with the Emperor. I begged him to be merciful. He promised me he would not kill you...

What???!!!

...he would only put out both your eyes.

61

I was horrified at this news. I had to escape! But outside the temple, the Emperor's cavalry lay in wait for me.

Man-Mountain! Wait!

Don't let him get away!

62

I ran for my life, heading for the shore. I had almost given up when I saw a dark shape floating just off the beach. One of the boats from the *Antelope* had escaped the wreck. I climbed into it and was carried away from the island.

For days, I drifted without food or water. At last, the wind and waves carried me to another island. My boat capsized in the surf and I was thrown out like a doll. With the last of my strength, I struggled to the shore…

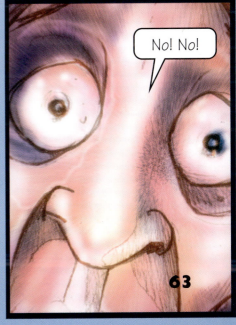

That was when I realized that my adventures were not over. They had only just begun…

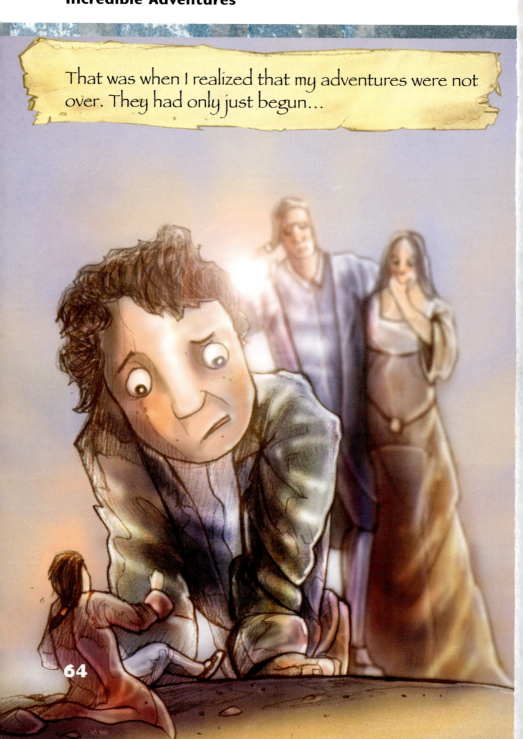